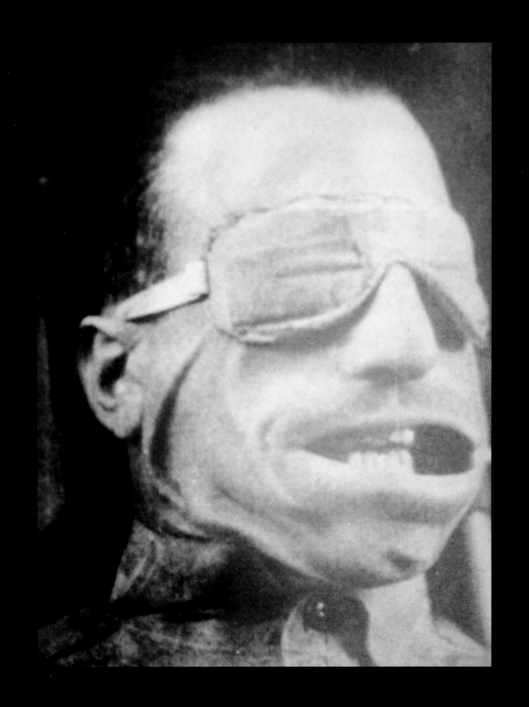

SNAKES IN THE COCKPIT

Images of Military Aviation Disasters

L. Douglas Keeney

MBI Publishing Company

First published in 2002 by MBI Publishing Company, Galtier Plaza, Suite 200, 380 Jackson Street, St. Paul, MN 55101-3885 USA

MBI Publishing Company books are also available at discounts in bulk quantity for industrial or sales-promotional use. For details write to Special Sales Manager at Motorbooks International Wholesalers & Distributors, Galtier Plaza, Suite 200, 380 Jackson Street, St. Paul, MN 55101-3885 USA.

Library of Congress Cataloging-in-Publication Data Available
ISBN 0-7603-1250-8

On the front cover: Ground fire of a B-52 at Loring Air Force Base in Maine.

On the frontispiece: A volunteer test subject is being hit by a 275-mile-per-hour wind during wind-testing.

On the title page: Another shot of the B-52 on fire at Loring Air Force Base.

On the contents page: Airpower demonstrations such as this are a rare sight in today's cost-conscious, safety-minded Air Force. Not so in years past. Here fifteen B-47 nuclear bombers join up for a formation fly-by during the National Air Show at Philadelphia, 1955.

On the back cover: *Main image:* B-24 Liberator, World War II. *Left image:* The DC-3 had ditched in three feet of water off Andros Island in the Bahamas. All eight on board were safe but confused and anxious. April 6, 1965. *Right image:* The crash of an F6F-3 Hellcat aboard the *USS Bataan* left a gaping hole in its fuselage, attracting curious deck personnel. 1944. Minor injuries.

Edited by Sara Perfetti
Designed by Stephanie Michaud

Printed in China

CONTENTS

INTRODUCTION

Between 1947 and 2000, the United States Air Force lost 13,626 aircraft to accidents at the cost of 15,856 lives. In one year alone, 1954, more than 900 aircraft were totally destroyed. In another year, 1952, a single-year record for fatalities was set: 1,214 airmen dead in accidents. In that same time period there were a mind-boggling total of 37,807 serious military aircraft accidents (called Class A or Class B accidents), and an untold number of minor incidents and injuries. (Naval aviation accidents during the same time period were just as dizzyingly high and every bit as sobering as the Air Force statistics.)

The truth is, military aviation is an extraordinarily risky business. In lettering reserved more for the announcement of a social dance than something as grim as this, an official United States Navy Web site has a page titled "Your Probability of Dying This Year." For the pilots of a fighter or attack aircraft that number in February of 2002 was an eye-popping 1 in 443.

As ghastly as this number seems, it nonetheless represents a precipitous drop from the disastrous years of the 1950s. In 2001, for instance, 21 Air Force aircraft were lost at the cost of nine lives. On the Navy side, 15 aircraft were destroyed at a cost of 17 lives. Dramatic improvements indeed but still a harsh occupational hazard for those willingly giving of their time and talents to the higher cause of protecting our nation.

Although talking about accidents might seem like a busman's holiday for military pilots who themselves spend countless hours studying them, such is the grist of bar talk wherever pilots gather. Odder still, books on mishaps (like this one), and films about them, are often best-sellers in the aviation community. Despite the incongruities, there are good reasons why this is so. The first is simple—accidents are never an end in themselves. The cover page to an accident investigation report for an F/A-18 Hornet crash said it best: "It is the mission of the MIR team to evaluate all possible factors and come to a conclusion that fully explains the circumstances that led to the mishap. Only then, when the irrefutable evidence is presented, is our investigation closed. The importance of this process cannot be overstated. Our results will guide manufacturers and aviators throughout the fleet for as long as the type and make of aircraft remains in use." Fully explain the accident, says the Navy, then make certain the causes are well understood by the rest of the pilots.

The Air Force agrees. Says the Flight Safety Center at Kirtland Air Force Base, the goal of the Safety Investigation Board, convened in the aftermath of any Class A mishap (an accident involving the death of an airman or the destruction of an aircraft), "is to determine two things: *Why* the mishap occurred; and *How* we can prevent the mishap from happening again."

Thus, in the strictest sense, the military views an accident as the beginning of a lesson learned. Look again at the Navy's MIR (Mishap Investigation Report). In it are the answers to three questions: Why did this plane crash? Were all of the aircraft systems functioning properly? And finally, what was the pilot doing? The answers to these questions are routed to every squadron in the fleet and dissected in the harsh light of day. Have it any other way and you doom others to the same fate as the pilots that just punched out.

Thus, in an odd but entirely symmetrical set of contradictions, accidents play an utterly vital role in the fabric of accident prevention. The detailed explanation of an accident's evolution (a term used to describe the sequence of events from beginning to end) is thus understandably vital in the ongoing process of pilot training. What went wrong? Why wasn't the pilot able to solve the problem? What was the time frame? Did the pilot have minutes, seconds, or just a fraction of a second to react? And if it came down to mere seconds, what could be done to save the next pilot in the same predicament? It may not be easy, it may be harder this way, but properly understood and dissected, properly applied, properly passed down through the ranks, properly communicated, properly visualized, accidents become the road map to accident reductions. To give but one example, the bold-faced items on a pilot's emergency checklist are in large part based on accidents. Bold faces are the fastest way out of a tight corner. Because they're easy to read they can save an inexperienced pilot from the consequences of, let's say, an engine flameout by reducing the relight procedures to the five (pick a number) essential actions. But never forget that behind the bold faces are the ghostly images of aviators whose accidents became the lesson learned.

Little wonder then that talking about accidents, talking about near misses, talking about the things that went wrong is officially sanctioned. Why is this? Because in the military there are far more close calls than mishaps, and sharing the experience, sharing the story of the flight that almost augered you in, while embarrassing and certainly not sparkling with the right stuff, could easily save another pilot. In fact, so true is this that openness is officially encouraged by every branch of the military's aviation communities. I'll give you an example from the Navy's ORM (Operational Risk Management) manual. The ORM manual was designed to help pilots brief contingencies that during a mission might cause an accident, however remote the possibility. The theory is that by briefing possible scenarios, possible solutions can be discussed, and if that

one-in-a-million scenario actually plays out, the odds that the pilot might survive are thus vastly improved. Consider this scenario: A Navy crew is departing on a mission. They will have to refuel midair but instead of refueling on a Navy tanker, they'll be refueling on an Air Force tanker. So what, you say? The ORM would "what-if" any number of potential mishaps. To wit: "The Air Force tanker climbs above 30,000 feet to avoid turbulence and weather. The tanker flies 50 knots faster than the Navy tankers normally fly. The F-14 has to use intermittent afterburner to keep up with the tanker, resulting in a compressor stall on one engine." Stall, spin, possible crash.

Or this: "The Air Force boom operator has never tanked with an F-14 before. He attempts to fly the boom to the aircraft's probe rather than fixing the boom's position. The boom hits and cracks the window."Each of these scenarios is in itself a serious in-flight emergency and each could easily evolve into a fatal crash. But by talking about the mere possibilities of such things one raises the odds of survivability, and that's the master that bar talk and hanger flying and ORM programs serve: survival in the air. If these had evolved into Class A mishaps, a pilot would be dead. Prevent them, and a pilot lives to fly another day. It's that simple.

Talking, thinking, planning, and sharing stories is part of the process that helps pilots survive. In the Navy, talking about close calls

is fostered under the aegis of "anymouse," which is a program designed to encourage pilots to speak up (and write about) their experiences. The name itself fosters participation. Says the official Navy history of the anymouse name: "Legend has it that the name Anymouse started out as a simple typo; someone somewhere didn't know how to spell 'anonymous' and didn't have a dictionary. Whatever the origins, [it was] originally intended as a means of encouraging flight personnel to make voluntary and anonymous reports of near-accidents and incidents which they might not report through established channels and formal reporting systems. . . . Any aviator desiring to report a situation merely takes a form and envelope from one of the attractive suggestion-type boxes available in all operating units. Anonymity is the heart of the system."

What a constructive, unintimidating way to bring aviators forward, and, evidently, with some success. Anymouse stories can be found pinned to bulletin boards on Navy bases and in numerous official Navy publications (and Web sites).

The Air Force encourages talking, too. A slip of paper given to pilots in Undergraduate Pilot Training bears this throat-choking quote. It says: "We should all bear one thing in mind when we talk about a troop who rode one in. He called upon the sum of all his knowledge and made a judgment. He believed in it so strongly that he knowingly bet his life on it. That he was mistaken in his judgment was a tragedy, not stupidity. Every supervisor and contemporary who spoke to him had an opportunity to influence his judgment. So a little of all of us goes in with every troop we lose."

This exhortation is invariably followed by the words of the Instructor Pilots who urge the budding aviators to learn to speak with each other. Pleaded one author from the Flight Safety Center at Kirtland "Do so at every possible opportunity. Crew debrief, formation debrief, flight safety meetings, bar talk. Set the example and encourage others to speak and share." Which explains why books and videos on accidents are bought and read by the pilot community. Here are the photos they never saw. Here are the accidents they've heard about but never seen.

That's the half of it. The other half of it is this: Then, as now, military aviation plays out on a stage not closely covered by the general

Crash-testing airframes.

media. Military accidents, when they happen, happen in a place we civilians don't occupy. I call it the parallel universe. Alongside our newspapers and magazines, the military has its newspapers and magazines. Alongside our grocery stores and department stores, the military has its grocery stores (the PX) and department stores (the Base Exchange or BX). The military has its own housing and schools, its own universities and hospitals, and even gas stations and fast-food restaurants. This is a life parallel to our own with a fuzzy, opaque membrane standing in between. We can see the military, but not clearly, and so our day-to-day experiences aren't shared. This is equally true for military accidents. Accidents are part of military aviators' lives (and their families') but by and large, the day-to-day military flight mishaps happen on the base and don't cross over to our side of the divide. When they do, when a plane falls to the ground on the civilian side, it's a moment made awkward by the contrasts in cultures. A military person stands in front of a smoking hole in a civilian neighborhood facing an inquiring civilian media and stiffly tries to explain it—it being the accident but "it" also being something finer and more subtle: the "it" that accidents happen and, well, *it's* an accident; we'll handle *it*; *it's* not good, but *it's* part of our lives; we've dealt with many more than this, so what's all the shock and surprise? Using this as the anchor point to his own commentary, Tom Wolfe wrote in *The Right Stuff*: "Sometimes, when the young wife of a fighter pilot would have a little reunion with the girls she went to school with, an odd fact would dawn on her; *they* have not been going to funerals." This is the divide: Military pilots and their young families have been going to funerals. Their friends who are stockbrokers and accountants have not.

And this is the other reason why many pilots keep books like this on their shelves. When it's over and done and they put away their flight suits, when they become civilians, even for a weekend, they get tongue-tied trying to explain their world. How do you explain the clunking, roaring, booming, snapping, screeching, oil-and-kerosene-filled flight deck of an aircraft carrier and the purple shirt that lost a finger and the brown shirt that was blown overboard and the two A-6 pilots that augered into the fantail in between the clinking of glass at a cocktail party during talk about lawn seed or the failed Enron partnerships? You can't, and pilots rarely do. Instead, say many, mishap photography does the job just fine. Hand them a book. Show them a video. Let the civilians see it without having to talk about it, they say.

In 1995 I published *No Easy Days: The Incredible Drama of Naval Aviation*. It was in many ways a report on the types and nature of accidents suffered by naval aviators. Seeing photography from aircraft carriers allowed non-military readers to view firsthand the seemingly endless ways a flight can go wrong. Ramp strikes. Shifting cargo during the cat stroke. Gear-up landings into the barricade. In-flight tailhook engagements. Engine failures. Accidental ejections. Too little pressure on the cat stroke. These were just some of the problems portrayed—the obvious problems, no fine points or subtleties involved. Did the book work? Did it part the curtain for even the span of a hundred pages? Judging from the letters, civilian and military, I think so. The book is now in its seventh printing.

Snakes in the Cockpit, though, is in many ways different from *No Easy Days*. What I didn't do in my first book was to delve deeper into that ever-so-slim margin that separates a hair-raising flight from a smoking hole in the ground. No, I don't intend to explore accidents and what caused them in this book: Many fine (and some densely thick) books have done just that. Instead, my interest is in the human factors, good and bad, that contribute to outcomes, an interest the Air Force and Navy share. You see, today's planes—versus those death traps from those oddly named "Golden Years of Flight," the 1950s, the years when more pilots died than any other decade of flight—are infinitely more reliable, more stable, and more prone to doing what they're supposed to do. Planes don't often fall apart. Engine failures are rare. But, as reports the Navy Flight Safety Center, in admitting the problem, "Naval Aviation's Class A flight mishap (FM) rate has declined substantially— halving each successive decade over the past 50 years. However, the proportion of Class A FMs due to human error has stayed relatively constant at about 80%." Human error.

The study of human error is the study of human factors, and human factors as the root cause of an accident is something that you can see throughout this book. But equally so, the human factor explains how pilots backed into an aeronautical corner without any chance of recovering without turning the situation into an accident (which by all odds it should have been). In fact, most of the accidents in this book were survived precisely because of human factors—to make it simple, they were survived because of good piloting. Bringing back a crippled aircraft is good piloting, and that is attributable to human factors. See the snapped tail on the B-52 on page 60. Until that bomber landed, no one would have bet a thin dime that any pilot could bring home a B-52 with so little of its tail left.

What then is the factor that pilots bring to the fore when they fly into a corner? There are many answers to that question—training, instinct, briefing contingencies, luck. But one term stands out and neatly wraps all of these factors into a tight bundle. It's called Situational Awareness, always capitalized, usually just called SA. What is SA? It's knowing where you are and what's going on around you while you're moving at 500 miles per hour. It's "feeling" the dynamics in a dynamic situation and being ahead of the game. I like the utter absence of any concrete meaning, but the utter clarity nonetheless, of the definition given by the Edwards Air Force Flight Safety Center in California: "SA is like sex. It is talked about in all flying circles, from the Aero Club to the squadron bar and even on the decks of 747s. We all know what it is, we know when we have it, some of us know when we are losing it, and all of us know when we have none (remember UPT and RTU?). SA may be the single most important factor that separates the great flyers from the average ones. Those that can maintain high SA throughout a flight will always be ahead of the game, drop bombs without getting shot, and take the first missile shot before the other guy knew what hit him."

In short, SA keeps a pilot alive. The pilot with good SA gets the missile off first. The pilot with no SA is a smoking hole in the ground. It's a hard concept to explain, so let me give you two examples from our side of the divide. Let's say it's an icy winter day. You're out in your car. You crest a hill and start to descend a winding road down. If you're like most people, you tap your brakes and skid, which quickly confirms your fears that there's ice underneath the snow. Your SA is good, so you slow down. As you go down the hill, you test your brakes and again, the car slips. You correct. You keep it slow. So far so good. But let's add a complicating factor. Coming up the hill is another car. You know the driver will try to gain a little momentum to make the hill but you also know that the centrifugal force of the curve could easily cause the other car to spin into your path. So now you have a dynamic situation. You're going down, potentially into an uncontrollable spin; the other car is coming up, also with the potential to spin. So you're alert. You're watching your own car, your speed, the road, the car coming up, and, if you're smart, you're also looking at the sides of the road to see if you have any escape routes. You put all this together—where you've been, where you are, and where you're going—and it's called Situational Awareness.

A destroyed C-141B dwarfs the firefighters who pull hoses in the foreground. This freak accident occurred at Pope Air Force Base in North Carolina in 1993. According to the Air Force files, an F-16D had a midair collision with a C-130 over the base and then crashed. The F-16 impacted the runway forward of the transport, then slid into it. The C-141 was unoccupied at the time of the accident; the disaster cost the lives of 23 airmen and injured more than 100. This extraordinary photo was featured in Airman *magazine.*

Another example. Professional football. Great wide receivers certainly have high SA. They weave through a blur of defenders, make their cuts, turn, look through the chaos of the scrimmage, the confusing screen of outstretched hands in the air; they feel the presence of the defender hanging on their shoulders and through it all, they somehow pick out a spiraling football and they see it as if it's in slow motion. Raising their hands, they go for the catch all the while "sensing" the positions of the defenders so they'll be prepared for the hit or, if they can, a fast cut up field for a few more yards. This is classic SA.

Situational Awareness is the thing that helps pilots stay alive when their flight controls are as limp as a snake. Pilots with good SA think fast. They reason through their options in a millisecond. They take actions and then try this and try that. SA is what helps them come out the other side with a solid stick and crisp rudder response. "SA is how we survive," says author and F-15 fighter pilot Jim Murphy in his book *Business Is Combat*. "SA keeps our brains ahead of the problems and lets us see options flash inside our skulls."

Options being the key word. Pilots like options. Opposite rudder. Pitch the nose down. Extend the gear. Punch in the afterburner. Try this, try that. Options. Options. Options. Pilots with high SA "see" more options than pilots with low SA. And when they exhaust their options, pilots with high SA

punch out before the ground swallows up their plane.

More often than not, most of the mishaps in this book were survived, some with incredible ease. On page 49 you will meet an F-51 Mustang pilot that flies three missions in one day, each coming perilously close to killing him, returning home on the second flight of the day with no landing gear. He smoothly executes a gear-up landing. He looks tired and beaten but he's unfazed; he has his cool. And then there's a C-47 pilot that executes a near-perfect ditching, and another successful ditching because an alert Coast Guard crew talks a passenger airliner down in the middle of an utterly calm Pacific Ocean. With just a fraction of a second to make his choices, Neil Armstrong punched out of a lunar test module before a pitch downward made survival all but impossible. Situational Awareness: it absolutely brims in these photos and is one of the hallmarks of great aviators. An F-4 Phantom pilot said it best. "There are a million ways a flight can go wrong and only one person to figure it out." How true on both counts. Just look at the Flight Safety Center. There are more than 100,000 crash folders at Kirtland Air Force Base and an equal number, I suspect, at NAS Norfolk. These folders tell the real story of how we conquered the skies.

There are several categories of accidents in this book, and each chapter covers one, save the first. The first chapter is on crash testing. In addition to the destruction testing that accompanies the development and ultimate acceptance of a new aircraft into the fleet, NACA and NASA routinely crash-tested fuselages to study how they break apart and, more important, what's going on inside. The subject aircraft would be accelerated (by sled, its own engines, or flown remotely) and crashed into the ground. To record the results, high-speed cameras would be arrayed around the impact area, and in the cabins. In almost all crash testing, crash-test dummies are strapped into the crew positions. These dummies yield life-saving data on restraining gear, the safest positions for the crew, and the cause of injury in a rapid deceleration (or acceleration, in the case of ejection-seat testing). Anthropomorphic in every respect, crash-test dummies present haunting images indeed. They look human, fly through the air as a human body would and, in the case of newer models, have weight distributed across their wood frames precisely as it is in the human body. The first section of this book contains some of the more heart-stopping photography from these tests, including photography that illustrates the torturous sequence of events that accompanies an ejection.

Following this first chapter is actual mishap photography. The accidents portrayed span the period from World War II to the present day and include almost every modern fighter, attack, bomber, and cargo aircraft in the fleet.

Here you will see some of the ways a flight can go wrong. Ditchings. Gear-up landings. Fires. Engine explosions. Accidents in bombers (which present their own set of problems, among them, crew coordination). In most cases, the pilots were fortunate; they rode it in and walked away, or survived the 300-mile-per-hour windblast of the ejection seat. Others, sadly, did not.

I tried to focus on interesting stories as well as interesting photography. To do that, I looked at photography at military aviation archives virtually across the nation—from the weapons testing grounds at China Lake to Edwards Air Force Base, California; from the Flight Test Center at Patuxent River, Maryland, to the National Archives in Washington; these, and the Pentagon archives, too.

ABOUT THE PHOTOGRAPHY

This book is the product of three years of research in military mishap archives. In sorting through the photography, I employed some parameters. I didn't want the book to be top-heavy with World War II, but I was interested in photography with good story appeal or unusual composition, and some of those were World War II images. The carrier shots, for example, are in many ways some of the most powerful images of naval air mishaps. The planes, like fallen birds, are hopelessly mangled, twisted back onto themselves. Still, the imagery is profound (and, thankfully, the pilots survived).

Likewise, I did my research knowing full well that cameras were often hastily pulled out and photos would often be blurred. I also knew that in many cases the very best photography might be accompanied only by the thinnest of caption or explanation. Try as one might, the full story was oftentimes elusive. Yes, the average public affairs officer or base historian will go out of their way to help you find captions, but when they're not there, they're simply not there. In the few instances where this was the case, the photography had to be terribly interesting or I discarded it entirely (see the burning B-52 on pages 67 and 68 as an example of a compelling imagery but little information).

As an aside I add this observation. The Internet has tempted far too many people to digitize photography and blithely discard the originals. Digital images are no panacea. Unless scanned at high resolution, detail is easily lost and with that, some of the "story" of the incident as well. Nonetheless, digital images have become so pervasive that in many cases the digital image is all that can now be retrieved. We could well do with tempering our infatuation with the Internet and being more concerned with the preservation of images in their original form.

That said, what of the name, *Snakes in the Cockpit?* "Snakes in the cockpit" is an expression often used by military pilots. As a civilian pilot, I can attest to the feeling it describes, for I, too, have had those bad days—days when the ailerons feel mushy and nonresponsive, days when the controls in your hand feel as limp as the body of a snake and the rudder pedals, its tail. That's what it means when you have snakes in the cockpit. Nothing seems to work. The flight controls are limp.

The message, then, is the same today as it was during the first years of flight: Military aviation is demanding, challenging, and sometimes unforgiving. Said one safety investigator at Kirtland, "Each of us as military aircrew run pretty close to the ragged edge of mayhem on a daily basis." As the following pages amply illustrate, pilots the world over, pilots through time, pilots in every branch of the services have had to suffer those ragged edges. When it happens, they use every ounce of their training—and more than a few quick prayers—to get down in one piece. Sometimes it comes down to something no more graceful than a controlled crash, but as we look at these photos, it is not inappropriate to remember the young men and women who take these risks so that we may sit securely in our homes certain in the knowledge that our skies and our borders are secure. On our side, at least for me, mishap photography deepens my appreciation for these brave men and women. No matter how invisible the statistic may be, our nation pays a dear price for freedom and safety—15,000 aviators since 1947. Twice that including the Army, the

Navy, and Marines. This book, a sequel to *No Easy Days*, illustrates the price. My goal then, as now, is to take readers into what I consider to be the most demanding flight environment in the world and in so doing, show them, through real-life photography, what few military aviators think about or talk about or even *want* to talk about but experience every day. Crash photography is unusual art, yes. But the message is one of tribute, of respect for the men and women who endure these risks.

We owe these aviators much.

—LDK

THE FLIGHT TEST FILES

Flight safety starts by preparing for the day an accident happens. Just as sure as pilots will fly, they will crash. Thus, while pilots train to handle emergencies, aeronautical engineers and human factors specialists study the aircraft to make them more survivable. Crash testing and crash-test dummies are the tools of their trade. In this section, photography from high-speed cameras shows some of the more unusual crash tests. The early photog-raphy, such as these photographs (all taken in 1951 and 1952), illustrates the first efforts to understand how an airframe collapses, how deceleration affects an aircrew, the frame-by-frame mechanics of the ejection or egress sequences, and other phases in an accident and how they might be made more survivable. The final crash test pictured in this section was a fuel test conducted in 1984—all together, 33 years of crash-test studies.

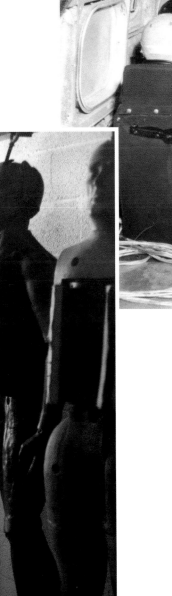

Above: NACA was one of the first agencies to use crash-test dummies. Inside the fuselage you can see that rather primitive dummies have been seated at various angles and are held back by various restraining devices, presumably to develop recommendations to improve the safety of C-82s configured to carry passengers. These tests were conducted at the Lewis Flight Propulsion Laboratory in Cleveland, Ohio, in 1951.

C-82

The National Advisory Committee for Aeronautics (NACA) was America's first flight-test agency and is the predecessor to today's NASA. NACA's projects ranged far and wide. Although the Air Force is widely credited with breaking the sound barrier, NACA in fact had its hand in Chuck Yeager's flight above Muroc Air Base in California. NACA was also heavily involved in crash testing and routinely studied the effects of a high-G deceleration (essentially a crash) on an aircraft. To gather data, countless aircraft were crashed at varying angles, altitudes, and speeds. Here we see a C-82 cargo transport accelerated into a berm. The left wing was designed to hit first and thus ground-loop the plane, which, as we see in the bottom row of photographs, it does.

FH-1 CRASH TEST, 1951

Impact survival studies, which is what crash testing was called at NACA, looked at the strength and structural integrity of the new fighter jets, too. In this sequence of photos, an early FH-1 is accelerated up an angular incline and cartwheeled across the impact area at Lewis. The jet hits the 22-degree incline at 110 knots and is momentarily airborne before impacting the ground, then rebounding again, tail high (bottom right). The nose section absorbs some of the initial G-forces as the jet begins to cartwheel.

This test studied the effectiveness of shoulder and lab harnesses—a then-novel design in pilot-restraining systems. To help the ground cameras record the motion of the test dummy strapped inside, the cockpit canopy was removed. Notice the plume of smoke coming from the jet's left engine in the photo below. The report notes that the cockpit was intact, although the FH-1 was "badly broken." It makes no mention of the "pilot."

Boeing 720 Fuel Test

The Controlled Impact Demonstration (CID). In 1984 the National Transportation Safety Board, along with NASA and the Department of Defense, undertook a study of a compound designed to reduce the flammability of aviation fuels. Often as not, a post-crash fire is as deadly as the crash itself. The hope was that a new series of fuel additives would reduce or minimize a post-crash fire, thus making an accident more survivable. Certain misting and coagulating compounds seemed to be promising, at least in the laboratory. But, as the CID tests so dramatically demonstrated, they were of no use. The crash was not as controlled as the designers planned (but what crash is controlled, anyway?), and the plane impacted the ground slightly off course at an undesired angle. When the steel wing cutters in the ground sliced open the wings, the initiators lit the fuel and a ball of flames ensued. The project was terminated, although not before it was given a few sarcastic names using the initials "CID," such as Crash Impact Demonstrator or Crash In the Desert. Notice the wing cutters in the ground as the CID 720 does a fly-by.

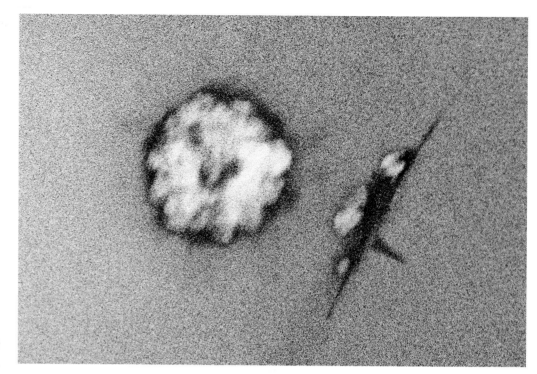

Surface-to-air missiles were proven to be effective without hitting their targets. These two photos were evidence that proximity explosions could take down a target as surely as a direct hit.

F-100A

An interesting dilemma faced then-test pilot Scott Crossfield. While on the first flight of a NACA F-100A Super Sabre in 1954, his cockpit lit up, warning him of an engine fire. Crossfield reacted (presumably shutting down the engine) but had to face a dead-stick landing, something even the engineers at North American, the aircraft's manufacturer, thought couldn't be done. The problem with a dead-stick landing in the F-100A was that the early F-100A had no flaps. Even using every bit of his emergency brakes, there was little chance he could slow the slippery Super Sabre before running out of airfield. Using the lake bed at Edwards Air Force Base as his runway, Crossfield lined up for a perfect approach, set down gently, and applied the brakes—but even with the vast breadth of Rogers Dry Lake, he was still sailing when he flew off the sand, up the ramp, through the front door of a hanger and, finally, through the side wall. However unorthodox, Crossfield brought his jet to a halt, walked away, and the F-100, which was damaged, was repaired. Both were to fly again.

EJECTIONS

Aircraft design is a science of balancing conflicting trade-offs. Speed for weight. Fuel for bombs. You can't have all of one without giving up some of the other. As but one example, attack jets don't have particularly large fuel tanks, lest they exceed their useful loads and be unable to carry bombs. Instead, they carry plenty of bombs but rely on tankers for air refueling.

Such trade-offs continue right on down to air safety. Military aircraft are volatile mixtures of fuel, hydraulics, bombs, weapons, and wings. Wedged in between is a human, probably the most important "system" in the aircraft. At some point, though, the trade-offs between weight, backup systems, and pilot safety come down to the ejection seat. If a pilot fully understands this, the ejection seat becomes nothing more than a flight system no different from the flaps or the landing gear. At some point, you use it. In fact, considering the abundance of energy sources that surround a pilot, ejecting is one of the basic ways to survive. Says the Air Force Safety Center: "Today the ejection seat is standard equipment in most fighter, attack, bomber, and trainer aircraft, and it's one of the primary means for improving aircrew survival."

That said, surviving the ejection is not always guaranteed. "During an ejection the limits of performance of humans and their equipment can be approached," says the Air Force, meaning that the wrenching, violent forces of the explosive seat charge and the powerful rocket motor often push humans beyond the threshold of survival. The data confirm this supposition. Between 1978 and 2000, the Air Force had 362 ejections, 92 percent of which were survived, a striking victory for ejection seats—yet still, 8 percent were not. The F-16 has had 238 lifetime ejections, with only sixteen fatalities.

In whatever small increments it may occur, reducing these ejection fatalities is a continuous process, and the primary tool is to sled-track-test new designs, new ejection angles, new explosive charges, new rocket motors, and new timing sequences. As the fol-

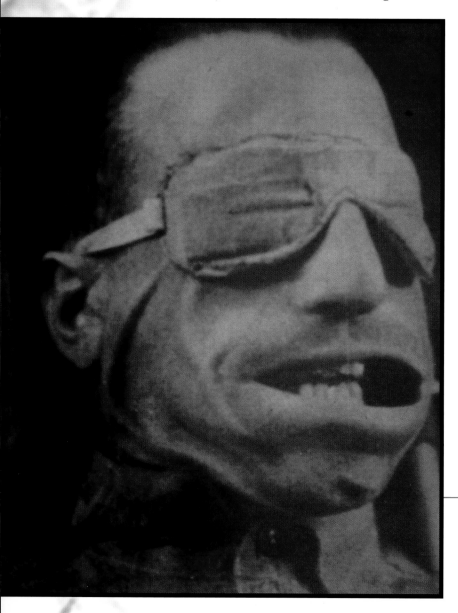

The 1949 airblast tests. Airblast testing was used to evaluate the fit of helmets and goggles, and to study the effects of high-intensity wind on humans. In this photo, a volunteer test subject is being hit by a 275-mile-per-hour wind. During this series of tests, pilots were subjected to winds as high as 350 miles per hour.

lowing photos document, an ejection is a complex sequence of events timed to microsecond synchronicity, and testing serves a vitally important role in making it all work. As an example, sled-track testing demonstrated that ejecting outside of a precisely timed sequence can result in a crew member being severely burned by flames from the rocket engine under the seat of the crew member ahead of him. Equally, if a pilot isn't in the proper position, the initial windblast can "easily lead to serious injuries of the arms and legs (due to flailing), as well as the head and face (as when the oxygen mask isn't attached)." All of which is assuming the pilot doesn't break an arm or leg striking the instrument panel or the canopy bow

on the way out, which is not an easy thing to avoid. One study determined that only 67 percent of the pilots that ejected from an F-16 got out without an injury (or with just a minor injury). The rest received moderate to severe injuries. What constitutes a "moderate" injury? Those 18 percent receiving moderate injuries were presumed to be mobile enough after landing to "move and evade capture" in a combat environment. The rest, 15 percent of all ejections, those that had a "severe" injury, suffered the loss of an eye or a limb, had a life-threatening injury, or were, on landing, incapable of moving. An important part of sled-testing is to reduce the rate of injury during the ejection process until it approaches nil.

The F/A-18's ejection seat is sled-tested.

Ejection seats are tested on high-speed sled tracks, one of which is located at Holloman Air Force Base, New Mexico. Realism is the key in such testing. Detailed mock-ups of each aircraft cockpit are mounted on rocket-powered sleds and accelerated up to and, if necessary, through the speed of sound. Using crash-test dummies and high-speed cameras, the ejection sequence is then closely studied. The designers want to make sure that the ejection was performed successfully—meaning quickly—with G-forces well within the range of human tolerance, and without the rocket motor from one seat burning the crewman behind it.

The entire flight envelope is studied in a typical sled-test program: Slow-speed ejections are as much of an interest to safety engineers as high-speed ones. In a slow-speed test, cockpits are mounted in the characteristically nose-high attitude of an aircraft on final approach, and accelerated down the tracks. The photograph at the right shows the trajectories of crew members during a slow-speed, multi-seat ejection, something that might occur, for instance, should an EA-6B Prowler lose engine power during a landing. Here the "crew" of four punches out.

Testing will at some stage involve a human subject. Here, one of the just four Air Force volunteers that tested an experimental ejection seat is being ejected from the crewman's seat in the lower compartment of a B-47. These photographs capture the first-ever tests of the then all-new downward-ejection seats. The B-47 was at 42,500 feet and flying at 500 miles per hour. After the ejection seat clears the aircraft, explosive charges will blow the seat away from the airman and the parachute will deploy. The new "downward" ejection concept would be a permanent safety feature not only on the B-47 but on B-52s, as well.

These Korean War-era photos show an actual, life-saving ejection from a combat fighter. The Mig in this gun-camera footage has been engaged by an American pilot and has clearly lost the battle: In this sequence we see the final moments. The flash in the second frame is that of the explosive bolts blowing off the canopy and the charge under the pilot's seat. The pilot stays in a neat bundle as he clears the tail and rockets to safety.

Over the years, the Soviets had developed some of the most innovative ejection seats in the business. Low-level ejections from the Mig-29 and the Su-27 at air shows have left more than one spectator shocked to see that any system could actually shield a pilot from high-speed windblast, much less that his chute could blossom in what feels to be no more than the space of a few seconds.

CHAPTER TWO

LANDING MISHAPS

Landings are the second most dangerous phase of flight—after takeoffs—and during this final phase of a flight, the pilot has little air left to play with when snakes invade the cockpit. The most common problem illustrated in the next section is a gear-up landing but as the following photographs show, even these come in a wide variety of flavors.

This B-24 Liberator completed its mission during World War II only to crash on landing. The crew scrambled to safety before the bomber erupted in flames.

F-84 THUNDERJET

A Republic F-84 Thunderjet, Turner Air Force Base, Georgia, March 1956. The foam on the runway hides just how remarkable this gear-up landing was. The pilot of this F-84 spent three hours trying to work down a stuck left main gear but failing that, he pulled up the gear and set up for a belly-landing. Entering a long final approach, he decided to try to ski down the runway on his empty pylon tanks. Using remarkable stick control, he was able to work his plan out. The F-84 slid to a halt entirely on the pylon tanks. An inspection revealed that the belly of the F-84 was absolutely undamaged.

Instead of landing his damaged jet on the runway, the pilot of this F-80 Shooting Star has chosen to set down in a rice paddy adjacent to the runway. It was not without complications. Coming in at 170 miles per hour, the plane hit the ground and bounced hard, rocketing back into the air, which you see in the top photograph. The pilot then eased the jet back down and, in the bottom photo, it has safely come to rest in the muck. Notice the hole in the side of the fuselage above the wing root and just under the letters "FT." This was the result of a direct hit by enemy tank fire. Despite the encounter, and the hard landing, the pilot was uninjured.

GEAR-UP LANDINGS: F-80 AND B-26

Enemy small arms fire hit the hydraulic system on this B-26 during a mission over North Korea. This photograph was taken a split second before an emergency belly-landing. None of the Fifth Air Force aircrew members were injured.

A US-2C Tracker makes an emergency landing after a main gear malfunction. Coming in on a foamed runway at NAS Cubi Point in the Philippines, the pilot used the tail hook to arrest during the landing then made a hasty egress (above).

C-53

On November 19, 1946, a Douglas C-53 crashed in the Swiss Alps on the Gauli glacier. All twelve crew members survived the landing but then struggled to survive while they awaited a rescue. They suffered for five days in the severe cold at 8,000 feet. They were ultimately rescued by a Swiss team flying a small Fiesler Storch. It took eight trips in the ski-equipped Storch to ferry the survivors down off the glacier. The code word "FINI" was stamped into the snow by the crew to identify the survivors to the search teams.

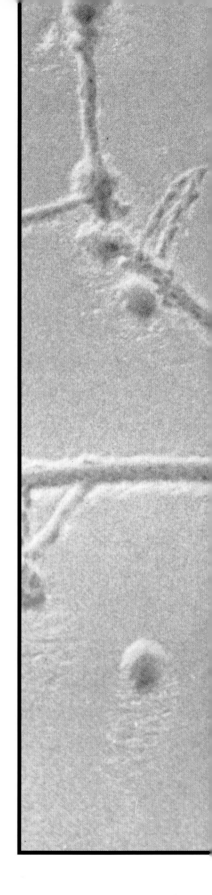

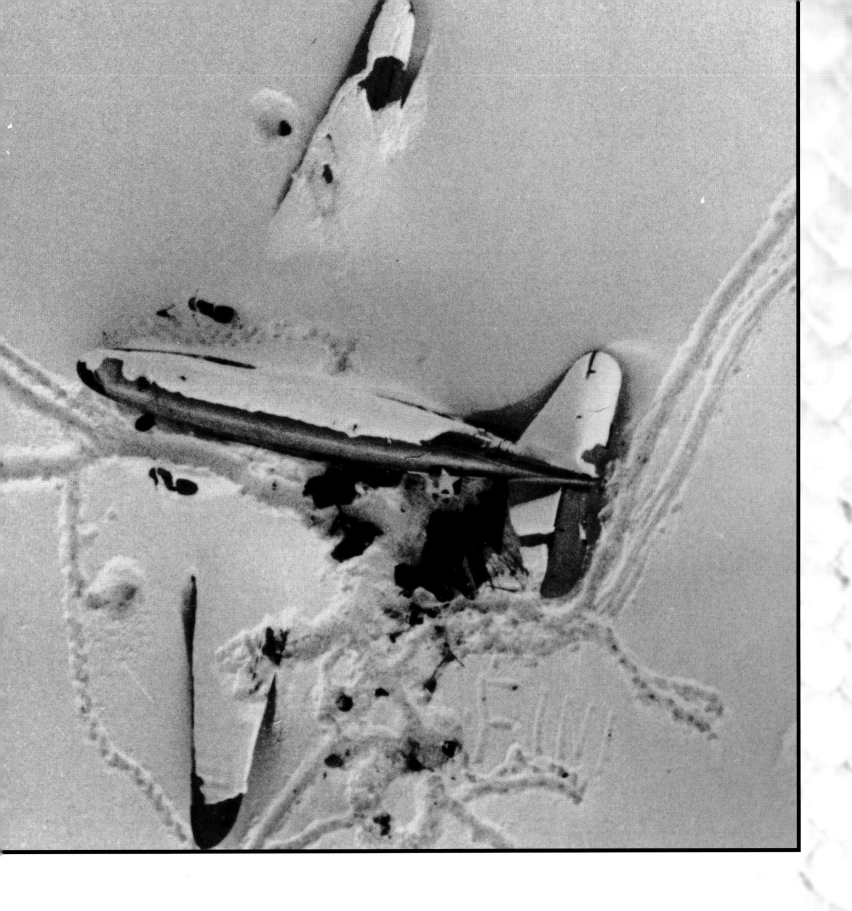

F-51 KOREA

Lieutenant Frank Buzze (right) of Syracuse, New York, was forced to make a gear-up landing after a strafing mission over territory held by the North Koreans, but that is only part of the story. This particular accident came at the end of Buzze's second mission of the day. The first ended little better. During that mission, a .50-cal bullet hit his aircraft and came to rest in the metal plate beneath his seat. Buzze landed, swapped aircraft, took his second F-51 aloft and belly-landed that one in. Still the story continues. Buzze commandeered a third F-51 and flew yet a third mission that day, this time coming back without incident. Showing an extraordinary sense of joie de vivre after it was all done, Buzze quipped, "my luck's getting better."

Lieutenant David Gray of Selma, Alabama, made the spectacular gear-up landing seen above. Damaged during a close-air support mission, he diverted to an airfield then in use by the 18th Bomber Wing. A quick-thinking photographer got this shot moments after the airplane's initial contact with the runway. Notice the bent tips of the four-bladed prop. Gray walked away without injury.

This F8K crusader takes a foam runway at NAS Guantanamo Bay, Cuba, after the nose wheel failed to deploy. This is one of the few color sequences that have been preserved in publicly accessible files. 1974.

In 1957, secret nuclear testing was underway in the desert north of Las Vegas, Nevada. The Army, Navy, Air Force, and Marines were there to determine which weapons systems could survive an atomic explosion, and what the psychological effects of a nuclear blast were on ordinary soldiers, sailors, and airmen.

Above, during the atomic blast STOKES, August 7, 1957, a Navy blimp plummets to the ground after the shock wave from the blast collapsed its tail section. The unmanned blimp was five miles from ground zero. Note the size of this blimp. Men can be seen examining the damage to the right and in the foreground.

NEIL ARMSTRONG'S 1968 LUNAR LANDING VEHICLE

The LLRV begins a rotation to the right.

On May 6, 1968, Neil Armstrong was strapped into a Rube Goldberg–looking contraption called the Lunar Landing Research Vehicle, a precursor to the landing module that actually put Armstrong on the moon. As this series of photographs show, though, the LLRV was difficult to control and this test flight ended in a crash. As the LLRV pitched forward, it lost power, and suddenly began to plummet to earth. Thankfully, it had an ejection seat. Armstrong quickly pulled the ejection seat chord and was safely blown free. His parachute opened just 50 feet above the ground. This series is interesting, and, no doubt historically significant among the stepping-stones to the moon, but it's also one of the few photographic sequences of an actual ejection during an in-flight emergency. You can actually see Armstrong's legs as he's rocketed upward and away from the vehicle (top opposite).

Foam coats the wreckage of the LLRV; burnt grass surrounds it.

M2-F2

Almost every American born between 1940 and 1960 in some way knows about this crash—the May 10, 1967 landing accident of the M2-F2. First some facts. The M2-F2 was part of NASA's lifting-body test program, one of the most promising yet unfulfilled concepts in aeronautical engineering. Essentially, the theory behind the lifting-body concept was that the body of an aircraft (instead of the wings) could be shaped to provide the lift, thus creating a whole new generation of aircraft with performance characteristics quite apart from conventional designs. The crash shown here, however, greatly contributed to the program's end. As the pilot, Bruce Peterson, made his approach for the landing, the M2-F2 suffered a pilot-induced oscillation (PIO). After recovering from the PIO, he was distracted by a helicopter in the air space nearby and drifted right, thus throwing the aircraft out of its intended lineup. The pilot skillfully corrected the flight path, but as he flared for the landing, the M2-F2 hit the ground before the gear was fully extended. The M2-F2 went wild. It rolled and tumbled and flipped and danced several times before finally coming to rest upside down in a cloud of sand and dust. It had all the earmarkings of a Class A mishap—a fatality. Incredibly, though, it was not. Peterson was severely injured but survived to make a complete recovery (alas, with the loss of vision in one eye). But why do we remember this accident? It has nothing to do with flight testing, aeronautics, or Edwards Air Force Base. This accident is immortalized because it was part of the opening sequence for a popular TV series in the 1970s called *The Six-Million Dollar Man.*

The Six Million Dollar Man *always began with the gut-wrenching footage of this crash. What really happened to this vehicle? This is the research plane called the M2-F2 after it came to a rest.*

The M2-F2 Lifting Body was carried aloft by a B-52. Here we see the M2-F2 mated to a hard point under the wing of a BUFF. 1966.

HEAVIES

Pilots of single-engine aircraft are in many ways blessed. When an emergency crops up, they have but one person to consider. Not so in a heavy. In heavies— bombers, tankers, and transports—pilots have crews of four or more to consider (as well as passengers, in the case of transports), which complicates matters accordingly. What works in an F-15 (punching out, for instance) may not be feasible with 20 airmen on board. Then there are the sheer physical issues of a 200,000-pound aircraft. Is it better to abort the takeoff and solve the problem in the air or will an abort cause the landing gear to crumble under the weight? Pilots of bombers and transports face far more than just the problems of solving the emergency; they have big, bulky aircraft to fly and an entire crew's safety to consider.

Aviation as art: Three B-47s paint their signatures against a deck of puffy clouds.

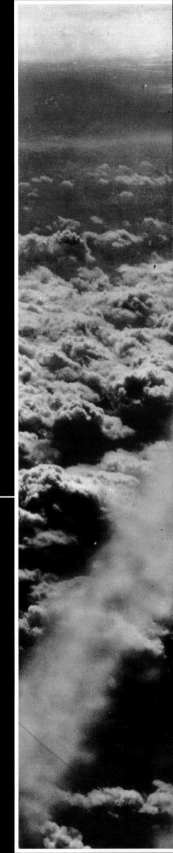

Emergencies in jets with large crews are complicated by the needs of the crews themselves. This B-36 is flying with a crew of 13 (but crews twice that size were common). In sifting through their choices, pilots dealing with an emergency while carrying a large crew have to consider the best option for the entire crew. Giving the crew time to get out is the usual choice.

B-36

Firemen crawl over this B-36 Peacemaker like ants, and like ants they are dwarfed by the giant props. It seems that the outboard starboard engines on this bomber were involved in a fire, but no detail was released with the picture. This is a late-model B-36, as the jet engines attest. The B-36 was woefully underpowered even with the six mammoth corncobs that pushed it through the air, so four jet engines were added to give it a little more go. Whatever the cause of this accident, engine problems plagued the Peacemaker throughout its entire service history. This photograph was taken at Carswell Air Force Base in Ft. Worth, Texas. 1957.

On January 13, 1964, a B-52 Bomber flying down the East Coast of the United States encountered a turbulent thunderstorm. The pilot communicated with the controllers, but there was no path around the embedded cells. The plane hit the worst of it. It pitched up and down and shook with a ferocity none of the crew had experienced before. In the midst of this, the tail snapped off and the plane crashed.

In the annals of aviation accidents, this crash would have been no more than a footnote except for two things: the B-52 was carrying nuclear bombs, and this wasn't the first time a tail had snapped off. The crash investigators recovered the lost bombs and then initiated a series of flight tests to examine the B-52's tail structure. During one of those tests—a flight through extremely turbulent up and down drafts along a mountain range—the tail snapped. Incredibly, the pilots brought this plane back home for a safe landing—a plane with no tail. This photo came from a camera in the chase plane. Late 1960s.

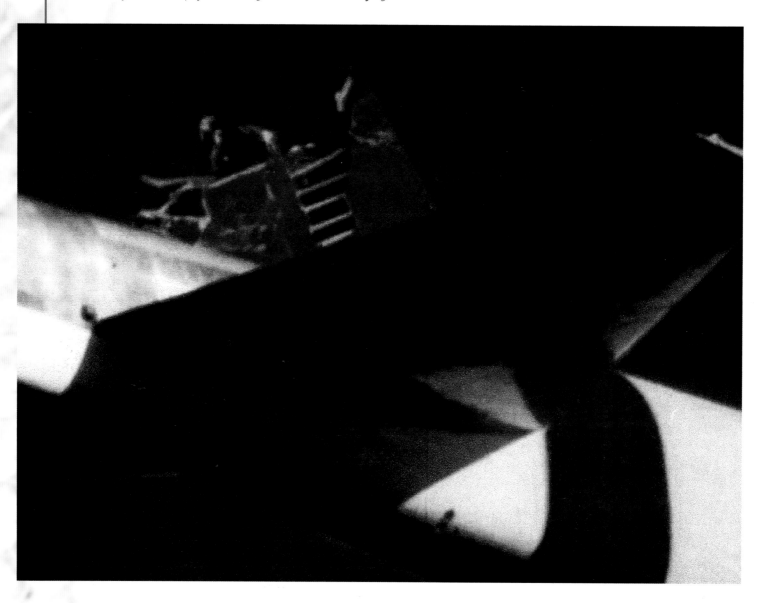

C-5A

The almost endless runway created by the hardpan of Rogers Dry Lake, Edwards Air Force Base, California, was the perfect place to land this C-5 with no nose gear. With the help of a chase plane, the pilot eased the Galaxy onto its mains, then gently lowered the nose.

This is one of the largest aircraft in the world. It can fly 70 tons of cargo thousands of miles away yet still take off fully loaded in 8,300 feet of runway. Four turbofan engines power the C-5. Each produces more than 43,000 pounds of thrust. The air intake alone is more than 8.5 feet in diameter.

Landing this Galaxy took particular nerve. The Galaxy has 12 internal wing tanks with a total capacity of 51,150 gallons of fuel—enough to fill six and a half railroad tank cars—but even empty, enough explosive vapors remain to turn any misstep into a fireball. A full fuel load weighs 332,500 pounds.

C-54 BARKSDALE AFB

In-flight fires are one of the most dangerous and feared of all emergencies. This Douglas C-54 made it down and successfully landed at Barksdale Air Force Base in Louisiana, but was gutted by flames despite the efforts of firefighters.

B-24 Liberator, World War II.

B-52 Loring Air Force Base

This dramatic sequence of photographs captures a ground fire of a B-52 at Loring Air Force Base in Maine (since decommissioned) on June 28, 1958. Foamite was used to bring the burning jet fuels under control, but the flames are still intense, the smoke is thick and billowing, and the wheels are clearly burning, but not deformed, when these pictures were taken. Few details about this incident were released. The bottom escape hatch is open, indicating the possibility that some of the crew egressed before flames consumed the fuselage. The B-52 had ejection seats, but, as the left photo clearly shows, no one ejected prior to the crash.

B-47 MID-AIR

One of the backbone bombers of Strategic Air Command during the Cold War, a B-47 makes a gear-up landing at McConnell Air Force Base in Kansas. This Air Training Command bomber was forced to belly in after the nose wheel failed to extend. Ordinarily, a nose-gear problem alone would not force a pilot to belly-land. Not so in a B-47. The B-47s had just two main landing-gear assemblies and the mains were in the configuration of bicycle wheels—one in front of the other, straight down the centerline of the fuselage. Pirouetting on a single main was not an acceptable option, thus the belly landing.

During an air-refueling training mission, a B-47 and a KC-97 collided at 350 knots and 15,000 feet. How did this accident happen? The B-47 undershot the refueling position and was chewed up by the KC-97's props. As a result, two of the KC-97's engines were destroyed. As a precaution, the crew of both aircraft bailed out but, as often happens, both pilots brought their planes home safely (if not the worse for wear). The tanker was from Smokey Hill Air Force Base, Kansas, while the B-47 was from Davis-Monthan Air Force Base, Arizona. The KC-97 landed safely at Luke Air Force Base, Arizona. The B-47 pilot was able to nurse his injured jet back home to Davis-Monthan. September 1953.

A C-5A comes to a stop and provides these dramatic photographs. Taken at Rhein-Main Air Base in Germany, this 1979 landing was on a foamed runway after a nose gear problem. This high-angle shot romances the smooth curves of the Galaxy, revealing the hidden beauty of this venerable transport.

The wreckage of this U.S. Air Force T-43A, which crashed on April 3, 1996, was carrying Commerce Secretary Ronald H. Brown and his delegation. Bad weather contributed to the accident. These photos were taken on a hillside approximately 3 kilometers north of the Dubrovnik Airport in Croatia. Investigators are sifting through the wreckage to determine the cause of the crash.

June 8, 1966. One of the greatest tragedies in Air Force history occurred on this wonderfully sunny day over Edwards Air Force Base, California. After the XB-70 Valkerie completed a successful test flight, it was decided to take advantage of the historic moment and photograph the experimental bomber with the entire line-up of its chase aircraft. A tight formation was flown but for reasons that have been subject to countless theories and endless speculation, some of them involving the suction of the air over the wings of the XB-70, the F-104 Starfighter, (on page 74) seen to the right of the bomber, flipped into and over the back of the bomber, shearing its right vertical stabilizer. The F-104 exploded and the burning wreckage fell away. The bomber continued in level flight for a moment before flipping over into a tail-down death spiral. It crashed into the desert floor (page 75).

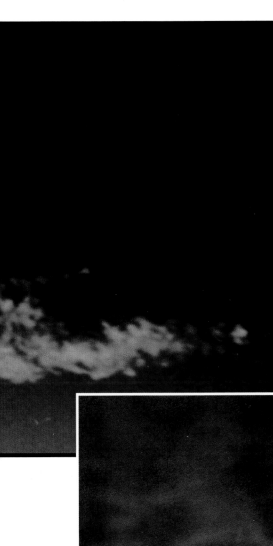

CHAPTER FOUR
DITCHINGS

While ditching seems to be a relatively "safe" option, crash-test studies and actual experiences demonstrate that ditchings are in many ways more difficult to survive than runway crash landings. Compared to a gear-up landing on a foamed runway, for example, ditching involves a more sudden and potentially deadlier deceleration. The G-forces of a water landing can completely destroy an aircraft and thus be as dangerous as a post-crash fire on a runway landing. Sinking is the next most common problem. Most aircraft will float, but only for a short period of time. Fires are also a problem even on the water (see the TU-16 on pages 80 and 81).

On the following pages, ditching is both tested and put into practice as military and civilian planes use the water for emergency landings. The standard procedure for ditching is wheels up, nose high, while landing parallel to the swells.

The random nature of an accident is illustrated with chilling clarity in this photograph. Shortly after takeoff from NAS Norfolk, this PBM lost power and crashed into Willoughby Bay near Norfolk, Virginia. All twelve members of the crew survived the landing—but not the aftermath. As it slid across the bay out of control, the PBM suddenly rammed into a reef of mud and nosed over. Seven men were trapped inside, all of whom perished. Those not trapped—five crewmen—escaped with only minor injuries. 1943.

B-17 DITCHING SEQUENCE

Although the B-17 was already destined for the boneyards (and soon to be phased out of active duty as a bomber), the Air Material Command at Wright Field in 1947 flew ten specially prepared B-17s to Eglin Air Force Base in Florida and ditched them into the Gulf of Mexico. Their purpose was to study the bomber's airframe to see how it might need strengthening. Why these tests so late in the life of the old Flying Fortresses? Following World War II, B-17s were being converted to fly search-and-rescue missions. They were modified to carry a lifeboat attached to their underbelly, which, like a modern-day drop tank, could be released and dropped to a vessel in distress. Caution dictated a better understanding of what might happen if the aircraft itself had to ditch. Thus, all ten of the bombers were modified to be drone aircraft and were remotely flown to watery landings. Some came in wing low, others, such as the B-17 seen here, executed dramatic, but picture-perfect, landings.

FINAL FLIGHT TU-16 BADGER

On May 25, 1968, the crew of the USS *Essex* watched in disbelief as a Soviet TU-16 Badger bomber swooped down from the skies and unexpectedly made repeated low-level passes alongside their carrier. In an instant, everyone knew the horrible truth: the Badger was in trouble. Adversaries or not, Cold War or no, no one likes to see a fellow soldier suffering a dire emergency. Yet here, out in the middle of the freezing cold Norwegian Sea, hundreds of miles from land, in the midst of the United States' antisubmarine training exercises, appeared the enemy, this twin-engined bomber—frantically dealing with an unknown, but life-threatening, problem. Panicky. Desperate. Sweeping past the carrier not just once or twice, but four times. Each time the men looked at each other, the sailors and the stricken aviators alike, neither knowing what to do for the other. Watching in utter disbelief, in almost absolute silence, with a queasy feeling of helplessness in their stomachs, the ship's crew knew one thing: The bomber was going down. And it did. It slammed into the water five miles away and exploded in a violent fireball. Why a fatal crash? Why not a gradual descent? Why four passes? No one knew. But when the *Essex's* helicopters circled the scene, no survivors were found.

Crewmen quickly snapped photos as the Badger made passes near the Essex.

Smoke marks the spot where the Soviet bomber crashed into the ocean. Rescue choppers from the Essex sweep the area looking for survivors.

DC-3 RESCUE

A civilian DC-3 was reported overdue on a four-hour flight from Haiti to Ft. Lauderdale, Florida. Air Force and Coast Guard search-and-rescue teams went into action and within two hours, they came upon this sight. The DC-3 had ditched in three feet of water off Andros Island in the Bahamas. All eight on board were safe but confused and anxious. Six were found standing on the wing while two had waded ashore to look for help—fruitlessly, as it turned out. April 6, 1965.

C-47 ENGINE OUT: NORTH AFRICA

On February 16, 1955, United States Air Force Major Granville Gore's twin-engined C-47 suffered a double-engine failure while crossing the Mediterranean between Tripoli and Athens, Greece. The major radioed his position and requested immediate assistance, then turned his attention to the sea conditions below. The waters looked calm, which was good, but they were over 100 miles from the nearest land. Clearly, a ditching was imminent. Major Gore readied his passengers as he glided toward the sea. Executing what had to be his best landing ever, Gore flared the C-47 and let the airplane's tail gently take the

first impact with the sea. Then, he lowered the nose, and the plane settled into the water. With an abrupt splash, the C-47 came to a halt and was motionless.

The successful ditching came about without any injuries, and the plane was evacuated in just three minutes. Incredibly, an SA-16 seaplane was on the scene as they landed and taxied toward the 18 relieved survivors. A crewman on board snapped these incredible photographs, surely the most dramatic images ever of an open-water ditching—and the graceful sinking of a classic warbird.

The view from the SA-16 seaplane. Two rafts maneuver away from the fuselage.

The forward door has allowed water to rush in, filling the forward compartments first. The plane is approximately 15 degrees nose down when this second photograph was taken.

The SA-16 has taxied around to the nose of the C-47 and, from that position, a crewman took these final two shots. Like the final plunge of the great ship Titanic, *the C-47's tail rose up in the air and then the ship slipped beneath the sea. A few seconds later, the plane was gone, and the surface of the water showed barely a ripple.*

SOVEREIGN OF THE SKIES

A Pan Am pilot with foresight, trust in his instruments, and a nearby Coast Guard cutter prepares to turn certain disaster into a remarkable rescue. December 21, 1956: The Pan American *Stratocruiser Sovereign of the Skies* developed engine trouble deep in the middle of the Pacific Ocean, en route from Hawaii to San Francisco. The number 1 and number 4 engines both conked out. Making matters worse, the Stratocruiser was low on fuel. Due to strong headwinds, there was no way to reach dry land—in either direction—on the two remaining engines. Luckily, down below performing weather patrol was the U.S. Coast Guard cutter *Ponchartrain*. It was 3:20 a.m. when the pilot made his decision to ditch. There were 31 passengers on board.

The aircraft and the cutter have now made radio contact. The pilot, Commander Richard Ogg, and the ship's captain, William Earle, devised a plan. The aircraft would attempt to stay aloft until daylight, at which time it would try to ditch as near as possible to the ship. The cutter would deploy water flares to create a runway. Here the Pan Am pilot makes a pass over the cutter as day breaks.

Inside the cabin, passengers practiced for the ditching while the pilot circled through the night, never going far from the cutter below. When the first shafts of the sunlight hit the waters, they could see that conditions were absolutely perfect. The aircraft descended. At 8:13 a.m., it ditched. The water was smooth and 74 degrees. Commander Ogg made a perfect belly landing, and within 20 minutes all of the passengers and the crew were safe aboard the Ponchartrain. One minute later the plane sank. The rescue is seen on the following page.

MARIN JRM-1 MARS

Seldom is a plane as rare as the JRM-1 photographed in a mishap that itself is as unusual as this one, but that is exactly the case with this series of fuzzy photos. This is the Mars. The plane pictured was but one of five production models of this heavy-duty seaplane. The Mars had its maiden flight on July 3, 1943. It was designed to serve the Navy as a long-range bomber but went through two evolutions before the Navy in 1945 ordered twenty built in the cargo version. Of these twenty, only five were actually delivered. The first of these crashed in August of 1945; the remaining four were assigned to NAS Alameda, California, and stayed in service until 1959. All except this one, the Marshall Mars, which in 1950 caught fire in Honolulu and was destroyed. Bits and pieces of the Mars can be seen sprinkling the bay as fuels explode and the Mars is blown apart. The JRM-1 was the largest flying boat ever to have been in service with the United States Navy.

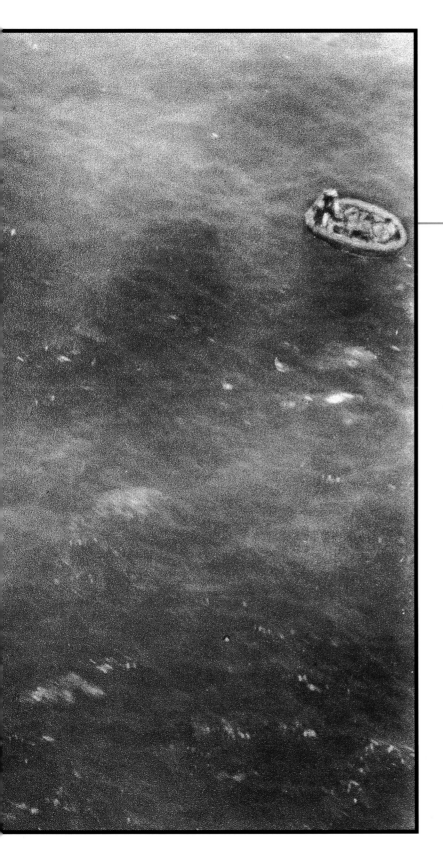

A true hero was made on this day in 1954. On July 23, 1954, Captain Jack T. Woodyard, piloting an SA-16 Air Rescue Service amphibian, rescued nine survivors of the British Service Cathay Pacific Airliner, shot down by Chinese Communists off Hainan Island.

Captain Woodyard and his crew were airborne soon after the airliner's dying radio operator sent a message that his plane was under attack and going down. Speeding to the area, Captain Woodyard was warned that the Chinese had ordered all military planes to stay away from the scene. In spite of this threat, he made an open-sea landing in 10-foot swells and motored toward the lifeboats. The survivors were in bad shape. They had been strafed by the attacking aircraft and all were injured. Nine people were hauled on board; one woman died on the way back to Hong Kong.

CHAPTER FIVE

AIRCRAFT CARRIERS

"The sole purpose of today's professional sailor is combat readiness. To respond quickly and decisively is the key to your profession. Every man injured or maimed in the performance of his duties reduces our ability to fight and is a needless waste of a precious asset, people."
—Foreword to *Flight Deck Awareness*, Third Edition, United States Navy

The perils of air operations from an aircraft carrier are well known by most readers. The antidote to these perils is relentless training, constant awareness of the potential for accidents, and extraordinary vigilance. Still, accidents happen: Indeed, rare is the "cruise" that completes its tour without a fatality or a serious incident.

Flight-deck mishaps are illustrated on the following pages. The photography in this section was selected to illustrate the most unusual mishaps—and their outcomes. One of these accidents, the fire aboard the USS *Forrestal*, dramatically illustrates the vulnerability of an aircraft carrier arising out of its confined spaces and the tinder-boxlike mixture of jet engines, aviation fuels, bombs, and the missiles that are in constant motion on the flight deck.

Other than the *Forrestal* fire, crewmen survived most of the accidents seen here, but each one involved some harrowing—and some embarrassing—moments.

A TF-9J Cougar dangles by its tail hook over the port side of the USS Lexington. Examine the picture closely and you will see that the aircraft extends from the water to the ship. 1966.

A freak accident goes down in Navy's history. The premature firing of a Zuni rocket during the launch of air strikes against Vietnam turned the flight deck of the USS Forrestal into one of the Navy's deadliest disasters. The wild rocket fired straight down the flight deck back into a gaggle of fully fueled, fully armed fighters and set off a chain reaction of violent explosions and fires. Making worse the tragedy, the intense heat from the fires caused several bombs to cook off and explode. The fire itself took 18 hours to extinguish and burned through several decks. The tragic accident cost the lives of well over 100 men. The accident has been the subject of several documentaries and training films, and led to a stiffening of flight-deck standards and rules, and even to the development of a more heat-resistant bomb casing. 1967.

The crash of an F6F-3 Hellcat aboard the USS Bataan left a gaping hole in its fuselage, attracting curious deck personnel. 1944. Minor injuries.

An F8U Crusader balances precariously in the catwalk on the USS Shangri La. 1968

This A4E Skyhawk veers hard to port when the left brake unexpectedly fails. The flight-deck chief tries in vain to halt the Skyhawk, but it continues toward the deck edge. Disaster, however, was averted. The A4's gear was caught up in the catwalk and brought the jet to a halt. Tail high, and with the nose pointed sickeningly down toward the water 60 feet below, she stops. These photographs were taken on the USS Shangri La during anti-submarine operations on Yankee Station, southeast Asia, 1970.

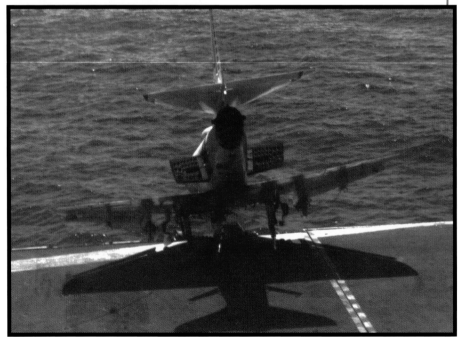

This series of photographs adorns the walls at the Flight Safety Center at NAS Norfolk. This is the well-known (at least in Navy circles) ramp strike of an F7U-3 Cutlass aboard the USS Hancock. It occurred in 1955 while the carrier was off the coast of San Diego. The LSO saw the lineup and knew the Cutlass was going to impact the deck edge just at his position. He sprinted across the deck, hoping to escape the crash (see the photo at the beginning of this chapter on page 97). Despite the surge of flaming gasoline, he escaped without serious injury.

An A4C comes in for a gear-up landing into the barricade. 1965.

"Hot Pappas," the red jerseys on today's flight deck, the fire and rescue crews, run to assist the pilot of a F3B Demon as it takes the barricade aboard the USS Bon Homme Richard. Why did the pilot need the barricade? The F3B bolted on its first pass but in the process, the right strut broke, forcing the pilot to land in the nets. The Demon was made by McDonnell and was the first swept-wing fighter off its production line. Only 239 of these aircraft were built, largely because it was so underpowered.

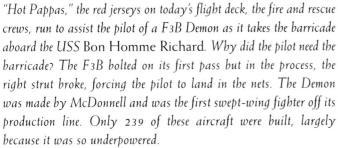

A Grumman US-2C Tracker takes the barricade aboard the USS Bon Homme Richard. The S-2 was an antisubmarine warfare aircraft. It was introduced in 1954 and, although retired by the Navy from active status long ago, today it remains in service with several foreign countries. The S-2 was a considerable aircraft to arrest in the barricade. It weighed 18,000 pounds: nine tons of screaming aircraft hurtling into a web net.

An F6F Hellcat comes to a stop against the carrier's island.

Flight-deck fires surround an A6 Intruder below and an A-1 Skyraider, left. The juxtaposition of these photographs provides an interesting contrast in the complexities of the egress systems of two eras. In the case of the Skyraider, the pilot had but to push back the canopy before scrambling to safety; however, in the case of the Intruder, the pilot had to fire the explosive bolts and violently jettison the canopy. Notice the plume of smoke tracing the path of the canopy as it blows past the tail. It is not clear from the information released whether the Skyraider or the Intruder were being maintained, preflighted, or taxied into a parking position after the landing.

F8U-1

This dramatic sequence captures a nearly fatal accident—a fatality that was prevented only because of the pilot's quick thinking. Coming in at over 100 miles per hour, this F8U-1 Crusader had its tail hook unexpectedly ripped off the fuselage as it caught the wire. What was for a split second a normal trap, quickly turned bad. Neither arrested by the wires nor flying fast enough to get airborne, the Crusader was now out of control. Speeding down the deck in a disorienting shower of sparks and flames, it aimed toward the angled deck. The pilot smartly elected to pull his face curtain, but only a fraction of a second before it was too late. You can see that as the pilot ejects, the aircraft starts to dive downward into the ocean. The canopy and the pilot blast free. As the aircraft heads the last 60 feet into the water, the pilot begins a backward flip in his ejection seat. The pilot was recovered and taken aboard the USS Franklin D. Roosevelt. 1961.

A C-130 seen from the round down of the USS Forrestal. 1963.

An F2H Banshee ramp strike. Miraculously, the pilot survived with minor injuries.

CHAPTER SIX

FIGHTERS

Fighter aircraft are fast, agile, rugged, durable, breathtaking and at the same time, almost always performing perilously close to the limits of their design tolerances. That said, they are loved by their pilots because despite the incredible mixture of seemingly incompatible demands, they are notoriously reliable. That reliability is just part of the story, however. Fighters are a clear symbol of power. Few aircraft project air power the way a fighter in full afterburner can. Indeed, just sitting on the ramp causes the heart in the chest of a

military man to quicken: Vipers, Eagles, Tomcats, Nighthawks, Rhinos-they all vibrate with the energy of a deadly force restrained inside even with the wheels chocked and the canopy down.

The photos in this section are about fighters. Fighters on display, fighters hunted down by missiles, fighters that curl around the smoke trail of the space shuttle in the aftermath of September 11th. Things happen fast in a fighter, good and bad. Some of both are presented herein.

An impressive lineup of North American F-100 Super Sabres at Nellis Air Force Base. This was the first fighter that could fly supersonic during level flight and in climbing, flight. It also holds the distinction of being the first supersonic fighter to become operational for the U.S. Air Force. 1962.

Several photos in this book are of things that the average person, military or civilian, just won't see again. For safety reasons, flying a large-scale attack formation like the one we see here is now the exception, not the rule. In 1962, however, when this photograph was taken, mind-boggling firepower demonstrations such as this one were fairly common. Here we see twelve North American F-100 Super Sabres in formation, dropping napalm canisters in what was called a maximum-impact release. Notice that several of the explosives have collided and have ignited even as they fall through the air. In combat, particularly during World War II, American bombers were hit by the bombs dropped by other bombers in a formation.

These two low-resolution images show two extremely dangerous conditions-engine explosions and fires. Of the two images, the burst of flames from the right engine on the Phantom is perhaps the rarest of all mishap images. It took luck and split-second timing to capture the instant of the fire. The F-14 Tomcat, its right engine having burnt through the afterburner cans, has already been abandoned but not yet approached by the firefighters onboard the ship.

F4 Phantom Inflight Engine Fire

F-14 Tomcat Engine Fire

The smoke trail of a Lark missile as seen from a helicopter hovering alongside the USS Norton Sound.

A sight certain to get a pilot's attention fast is the smoke trail of an air-to-air missile. Today, air-to-air missiles in the Air Force's inventory include the radar-guided AIM-7 Sparrow (which brought down 22 Iraqi jets during the Gulf War), the AIM-120 AMRAAM, and the ubiquitous, supersonic AIM9L. The AIM9 was developed by the Navy in the early 1950s and was adopted by the Air Force in 1953 thus becoming the de facto air-to-air missile of choice for the U.S. military. What makes the AIM9's current version so lethal is that it corrects problems that made the early AIM9s (and thus, by inference, their Soviet counterparts) easier to defeat. To give but a few examples, the AIM9's smoke signature has been reduced at least twice, thus lowering a pilot's ability to get a visual ID on it as it seeks out his aircraft. The AIM9, which, incidentally, is a heat-seeking missile and thus could not originally be fired head-on, now has optical sensing capabilities that let a pilot fire it from great distances, and fire it head-on. Perhaps most discouraging to the enemy, in the dry language of an Air Force fact sheet, the AIM9 is pretty hard to confuse by using flares or by hiding against the ground. Says the USAF, it now has "improved defense(s) against infrared countermeasures (and) enhanced background discrimination capability." You can run, but you can't hide.

The series of air-to-air missile photography in this section traces from the earliest land-launched surface-to-air missiles through an F-16-launched AIM9 going up the tailpipe of a drone F-102-up to the nuclear air-to-air missile. Missiles, as these photos show, can be effective without hitting the engine. Indeed, some air-to-air missiles will take a plane down with no more than a proximity explosion-the heat and/or the concussion being enough to destroy an aircraft if the missile explodes close by.

Pilots can defeat missiles. Pilots dogfight a missile the way they dogfight the enemy. Moreover, pilots know a missile's shortcomings, so even if an enemy fires one upon it, it is far from assured that the missile will take down its target. Some missiles can be outrun. Some can be out-maneuvered. Most can be outturned. And even if a plane is hit, the explosion is not necessarily enough to bring the plane down. At least two F/A-18s were hit in the engines by shoulder-launched missiles during the Gulf War, but both flew home as if it had been a mere bite by a mosquito. The afterburner cans and just the general toughness of today's attack/fighters make anything less than a full-up missile like the AIM9 almost useless. These photos were taken from high-speed cameras as test missiles were fired against drones. The results speak for themselves.

The deadliest missile ever flown by the Air Force was fired but once-the Genie air-to-air nuclear missile. This weapon was based on the theory that attacking Soviet bombers would be bunched up in the tight bomber formations seen during World War II. A nuclear warhead on the tip of this missile would explode and generate a shockwave so powerful that all aircraft flying within a half-mile of its detonation would be destroyed. These photos are from the first and only test firing of Genie-a successful firing, at that.

A Phantom goes home. A sense of loneliness suffuses this quiet but beautiful photograph taken against the backdrop of the high desert in California. An F-4 drone Phantom (QF-4B) takes a solitary ride home slung underneath a Marine Corps CH-53 Super Stallion. It is being airlifted out of the Pacific Missile Test Center at Point Magu on a chilly day in November of 1990. It survived a missile hit to its tail feathers, landed anyway, but now is headed to the repair shop-or to the boneyards.

This is a very powerful and certainly historic photograph. An F-15 Eagle flies combat air patrol above Florida. In the background, the space shuttle lifts off. What makes this photograph special? This was the first shuttle launch following the September 11, 2001, bombings of the World Trade Center and the Pentagon.

REFERENCES

Donald, David and Jon Lake. *Encyclopedia of World Military Aircraft*. AIRtime Publishing: London. 1994

Approach Magazine, Naval Safety Center, Norfolk, Va.

Operational Risk Management, Naval Safety Center, Norfolk, Va.

Tom Ganse, LCDR, USN, investigating the F/A-18, Naval Safety Center, Norfolk, Va.

D'Amore, George LTC, USAF, "USAF Aces II Ejections and You, the Aircrew," *Flying Safety Magazine*, HQ, Air Force Safety Center, Kirtland, N.M.

Will, Christopher, Capt, USAF, "Privilege: The Cornerstone of Flight Safety," *Flying Safety Magazine*, HQ, Air Force Safety Center, Kirtland, N.M.

Fact Sheet, Air Combat Command, Public Affairs Office; Langley AFB, Va.

GlobalSecurity

Boyne, Walter. *Beyond the Wild Blue*, Simon & Schuster, New York

NTSB Aviation Accident Statistics

DefenseLink News

Dryden Research

Headquarters, USAF

U.S. Navy Office of Information, "A Brief History of Aircraft Carriers, the USS *Forrestal*"

Boeing

Elevon-Aviation on the Internet

Air Material Command

Headquarters, Marine Corps

PHOTO CREDITS

Author's collection

The National Archives, Silver Springs, Md.

The Department of Energy Archives, CIC, Las Vegas, Nev.

Headquarters, The United States Coast Guard, Washington, D.C.

Edwards Air Force Base Photo Gallery

U.S. Naval Safety Center, NAS Norfolk, Va.

Dryden Research

DefenseLink News

Headquarters, USAF

Don Farmer

NAS Patuxent River, Md.

NASA

U.S. Coast Guard, Headquarters, Washington, D.C.

China Lake Air Warfare Center

INDEX

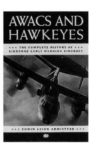